This Atmosphere of
Love

D0324508

This Atmosphere of Love

Franklin Bass Jr.

authorHOUSE®

AuthorHouse™
1663 Liberty Drive
Bloomington, IN 47403
www.authorhouse.com
Phone: 1-800-839-8640

© 2012 by Franklin Bass Jr.. All rights reserved.

No part of this book may be reproduced, stored in a retrieval system, or transmitted by any means without the written permission of the author.

Published by AuthorHouse   10/08/2012

ISBN: 978-1-4772-7632-7 (sc)
ISBN: 978-1-4772-7631-0 (e)

Library of Congress Control Number: 2012918375

Any people depicted in stock imagery provided by Thinkstock are models, and such images are being used for illustrative purposes only.
Certain stock imagery © Thinkstock.

This book is printed on acid-free paper.

Because of the dynamic nature of the Internet, any web addresses or links contained in this book may have changed since publication and may no longer be valid. The views expressed in this work are solely those of the author and do not necessarily reflect the views of the publisher, and the publisher hereby disclaims any responsibility for them.

I would like to thank my special lady for all the encouragement and being there for me and helping me through this process.

Softness Interlude

When sitting around you, I can feel a softness interlude,
With the dimples of your smile, this I cannot exclude.

A mark of time, brings the sweet smell of your perfume,
I get a delightful sniff, and I am consumed.

You are unique in every way, that passion you wear,
Shows itself in all of it's magnificence, makes me want to share.

Being that I'm aware of this way to feel, I resign myself,
To believe in softness interludes, to collect and store on my shelf.

7-17-09

Flowers all over the place

There are flowers all over the place,
Each and every time you enter my space.

They are different colors and styles,
All of them with bright summery smiles.

On them is a nice shimmery dew,
They all have the same personality . . . you.

So when I daydream or, see your pretty face,
I see and feel, flowers all over the place.

Vacancy

There is a vacancy in my heart,

For the lady who can give it a jumpstart.

I've been down this road before,

It's really becoming a bore.

Rejection, dejection, lies and humiliation;

I certainly hope that I'm not casting that kind of reflection

If there is a female out there, who is willing to take up

residency in my heart,

Without playing games that some of them start;

I will be taking applications in a little while

From those who can make me smile.

My miracle of Love

From the top of her head, to the bottom of her feet

I saw that she was the one, I was to meet.

When she gives of herself it's easy to tell that,

She's not placing my love on a shelf.

She takes care of home first, always helping me prepare for

the worst.

When I feel my world is crashing down,

She more than lets me know that she's around.

This is my lady, full of fire, the caring soul, the one that I admire.

She's my right hand, my velvet glove, my miracle of love.

8-08

Careful my love

Careful my love, I just might fall for you,

You are the one who may turn my gray skies blue.

To me your heart is to be admired,

It is of sheer beauty, no wonder why you so desired.

My Nubian queen, my lover, my mate,

I feel so blessed that I'd asked you on that first date.

In closing this poem I feel, I should thank you for keeping it

so real.

8-08

Delightful Melody

I feel you, indeed, I observe the inner beauty of you

I notice the charm, the smartness you possess.

The way you handle things, with the utmost Finesse.

The smell of your perfume, The way it entices me to Enter
your room.

Then I patiently wait for your Love, which you bestow on me
like a fitted glove.

This is why I say you are a delightful Melody,

You in your own way complete me.

8-08

Elevation

When you are in my presence, I am elevated to a higher level.

This kind of love has no comparison, It's the feelings you

cannot buy or sell.

There's magic in your style, the way carry yourself, makes

me smile.

The softness of your skin, the tone of your voice,

Leads me to believe that I am your choice.

So ask me if I'm elevated today,

I can tell you that you are my love every day.

8-08

THAT CERTAIN SOMEONE

There's a person soft and sensual, that came into my life, I
want her to know with all of my heart,
That she makes the difference, she's so caring, it's like I
wanted her from the start.
From day one, I could tell she was made for me, in my
dreams I see her smile,
Every now and then we come from different parts, and
dance for a while.
When we talk, we talk with each other, no raised voices,
We demonstrate education, because we know as adults
we have choices.
We feel that we are leaders in our community, a team of
lovers, if I may,
When it comes to what's best for us, we both have the final say.
So guys when you go searching for a soul mate, make sure,
you get the one
Make sure you get, at the end of the day, that certain someone

7-25-09

Only For You

When I say that I will be true,

Then without a doubt believe, it's only for you.

When I say it's beautiful outside, that the air smells sweet,

I say that to mean, the way you look and dress, is so very neat.

You never mask your personality, to spare my feelings or

neglect to say,

The things that are on your mind, that may bother you in

that way.

If I am troubled or terribly annoyed,

You talk to me to queel my anger, to null that void.

So when I say to you that, this love we can always renew,

Please remember that, it's only for you

9-21-09

Your Love Has Entered

Your love has entered me through osmosis,
I feel well again, it must be a new diagnosis.

It has entered my home as if like family,
I am happy, this must be my destiny.

Your love has entered the very air I breathe,
It's a great feeling, it shows that you're all I need.

Your love has entered me in such a nice way that,
I know I'm in Love, and I know I'm on the right track.

9-29-09

What I see when I look at You

I see a lot of charm and elegance,
A lovely form, a natural beauty, easily seen from a glance.

I see the sweet morning dew on her.face,
I can't find that prettiness any place.

I see doves sitting on a limb, singing sweet songs,
As I watch you grin, as we walk along.

I see the storms set aside as you enter towards my room,
These things I see, when I look at you.

9-29-09

My four leafed Clover

You are my four leafed clover, I love you many times over.

Passion is on my mind, that makes you truly a lucky find.

When we get snowed in, I think of our past summer and grin.

I always wanted to be in love, to be true and stay above.

I found that I can do great things with you, my constant lover,

My companion, my heart, my four leafed clover.

10-2-09

Much love to You

Much love to you lady of my dreams,
We're a perfect match, good together it seems.

The pleasantness of my day, has your name all over it,
I would run miles to get to you, I'd run hard, I will not quit.

You fascinate me with everything you say and do,
I am your Champion, I love you tremendously too.

You make me feel up when I'm feeling sad,
When there's a happy point in my day, I know it's you and
I'm glad.

When things fall apart and turn to goo,
I imagine your eyes and say, much love to you.

1-19-10

I feel You

I feel you in every way,
You are the essence of my every day.

You are in a great mood most of the time,
It is one of the things about you, that helps me compose
this rhyme.

I believe your heart is one that everyone should have,
It's like you are rubbing me with some soothing salve.

I know that when ever I am feeling blue,
That you are there for me, and I feel you.

1-19-2010

The happiest man of all

I can sit, stand or just be in one place,
I would be mesmerized by imagining your lovely face.

I can envision you smile any given moment, in any way,
During sunup or sundown, at any time of the day.

I see you as a nurturer, who loves to give of herself,
I am one of the lucky ones that you make sure, is in good health.

I find you classy with no ends or bounds,
I am happy to walk and talk with you on the same grounds.

Knowing how you love me, I can really stand tall,
For I am certainly the happiest man of all.

4-9-10

I envisioned someone like you

It started when I was in my late teens,
I worked on cars dressed in my farmer jeans.

Pretty young ladies smile as they walk by my shop,
A few years later, the rate of my luck began to drop.

Just when I though I could really give up on love,
I had a vision, a revelation, like right from above.

That was when I dared to seek out some person of new,
With all the love you give, I realized, I envisioned someone
like you.

11-27-11

Magic Flower

As the dawn brings new light and insects all buzz,
This new beginning shows a new day with you, better than
it ever was.

You blossom into a tulip, one of the nicest flowers I've seen,
Be I am with you in this image of love, this is a great dream.

I find you strong yet delicate to the touch,
You show me how much you care, that's why I love you so much

You have made me strong and wise, you've given me the
power,
To dedicate my life to you, you are my Magic Flower.

For Charlotte,

7-8-12

Growing Together

Getting to know you has been an exciting journey,

Seeing how you accept me for the who I really am, lets me

know that I am worthy.

During the course of the day, your smile fills me to the point

of satisfaction,

I know that in this relationship, I have taken the proper

course of action.

You bring love my way, as earnestly, as lightly as a feather,

For those reasons, I'm glad we are growing together.

4-24-10

My Dear Charlotte

As I am here contemplating my life,

I am thinking about a woman of whom, may one day be my wife.

She's sharp, witty, and beautiful all time,

When she enters into my zone, it seems as though I hear a pleasant chime.

The magnitude of her love, wraps itself around me in such a way,

It helps the start of a brand new day.

So if you see me smiling, you can surely bet,

That I am thinking about my dear Charlotte.

You Wet My Appetite

While eating a plate of sushi, I long for the main course,
It's not the other foods, I want, I crave you and your love in
full force.

You taste wonderfully delicious to me, a warm welcome treat,
As my prime choice, you satisfy me, and are the sweetest
of sweets.

When you set my dinner before me, I know it's prepared right,
That is one of a billion ways, as usual, you wet my appetite.

To Charlotte

8-1-12

Proof that I am in your heart

While traveling through the course of my day,
I think of the love and joy that you bring my way.

I also see that you wouldn't do this just for any guy,
More than likely, you'd kick them far off to the wayside.

When you come home after a day of hard work,
You bring me a kiss and a story of a friend or, an uncouf jerk.

As I sum up this note, not necessarily from the start,
I know you really care for me, that's proof that I am in your
heart.

7-19-12

Healing of My Heart

I was feeling down and quite lonely,

You came into my life and became my one and only.

You gave me the kind of love that I was missing,

Each day I daydream, and imagine that we're kissing.

My other relationships went sour, and all fell apart,

Then I met you, pretty lady, the beginning of the healing of

my heart.

To Charlotte

7-11-12

Sweet as Honey

It's said that sugar is the sweetest, even some caramel,
I've tried a lot of goodies, to pick the best, it's hard to tell.

Natural fruits and some chocolates can be fun,
The food that I crave, will have me dancing in the sun.

All assortments of candy taste real fine,
My choice is not just good, but of the very best kind.

When I go into the candy store, that's where I'll spend my
money,
On my beautiful lady, because she's as Sweet as Honey.

7-19-12

It's quite Simple

You are a wonderful person, very kind and unique,
I'm glad that I met you, getting your love was quite a feat.

Gladness is in my heart day in and day out,
It's because of your loving way, without any doubt.

I am wearing a smile, looking at your dimples,
Enjoying the love you give, clearly, it's quite simple.

To Charlotte

8-1-12

The Value of Our Love

The value of our love cannot be measured by numbers,

One way to record it is, by noticing people observing in wonder.

The harmony we have strived for has been attained,

Joy is the result, at this pace, it will always be maintained,

You and I have a deep connection, we fit like a glove,

I am quite inspired that others can see the value of our love.

To Charlotte

8-1-12

That Tender You

You demonstrate the true definition of love and sharing,
That I want to have you by my side forever, I am that daring.

Your smile exudes kindness and understanding,
You help me stay sure footed, reminding me of where I'm landing.

We work together while close or apart, that's what we do,
As all this is transpiring, I can certainly see, that tender you.

To Charlotte

8-1-12

Smile All Around

I sense that when we're together, the sun becomes bright,
As we stroll through the neighborhood, the birds take to flight.

People are more lighthearted, they have kind words to say,
Frequently this comes to my mind, I wouldn't have it any
other way.

The things that are happening, I say, cannot be found,
Proof emerges as we walk and see that there are smiles all
around.

To Charlotte

8-1-12

Mirror Mirror

I see the reflection of myself, standing very tall,
When I met you I became excited, we were having a
happy ball.

Lasting as long as it has, is truly amazing, well worth the time,
I cherish this experience as a trail to the mountains that
aren't hard to climb.

Each time I look into your eyes, the message is clearer and
clearer,
You are here for me and that makes me smile and say
Mirror, Mirror.

9-8-12

I Cherish the Flowers

Some guys might not notice the fairness that I see,
It is the beauty of the kindness and the natural goodness
that be.

I am not surprised by the emotional balance that weighs in,
It really gives off a sense of pride, knowing I am on the side
that wins

The feminine side of the world contains the best powers,
As an admirer of these persons, I cherish the flowers.

9-8-12

A Certain Lovelyness

From what I have observed, the ladies possess a lot of pride,

They won't always tell if they are lacking anything, they
keep that deep inside.

They are wise, some beyond their years,

Enduring many hardships and struggles, I hate to see them
in tears.

A woman will put herself together well, most times with a lot
of fuss,

To create the inward and outward of a certain lovelyness.

9-8-12

A Man's Dream

To conversate with a lady, her recognizing that's what she is,
Working together toward the same goals, ever reminding
him, that she is his.

Helping him through some of the most perplexing puzzles of
the day,
Realizing that he concentrates on one thing at a time,
that's him, that's his way.

She should know that a man likes working as a team,
He wants the same lady that he fell in love with, that's a
man's dream.

9-8-12

I'm not Surprised

It's cause for concern, to think that we almost didn't meet,
I'm really glad we did, oh baby, what an awesomely cool treat.

You have my best interests at heart, this I will not deny,
My thirst for love has been quenched, you fill it without
strain or try.

Joy is what I feel, I soar, my heart is supersized,
Being with you is the happiest part of my life, certainly I'm
not surprised.

> To Charlotte

8-12-12

Filling that empty Void

We're building our lives together, that's a good thing,
While sharing our love, I can't wait for what the next day
may bring.

There is true love in your heart, I admire you for that,
We go through our day helping each other, leaving no
room to spat.

When I am feeling troubled or when I got annoyed,
You comfort me, supporting me, and filling that empty void.

To Charlotte

8-12-12